WILD Nature & Animals
ADULT COLORING BOOK

20 CALMING DESIGNS TO COLOR
BEARS, OWLS, FOXES AND MORE!

Illustrated by Liz Emirzian

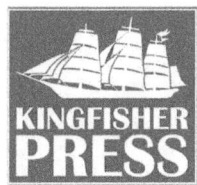

KINGFISHER
PRESS

Cover Art by Liz Emirzian

Printed by: Createspace.com
10 9 8 7 6 5 4 3 2 1

Kingfisher Press
www.kingfisherpressbooks.com
March, 2016
New York, New York, USA

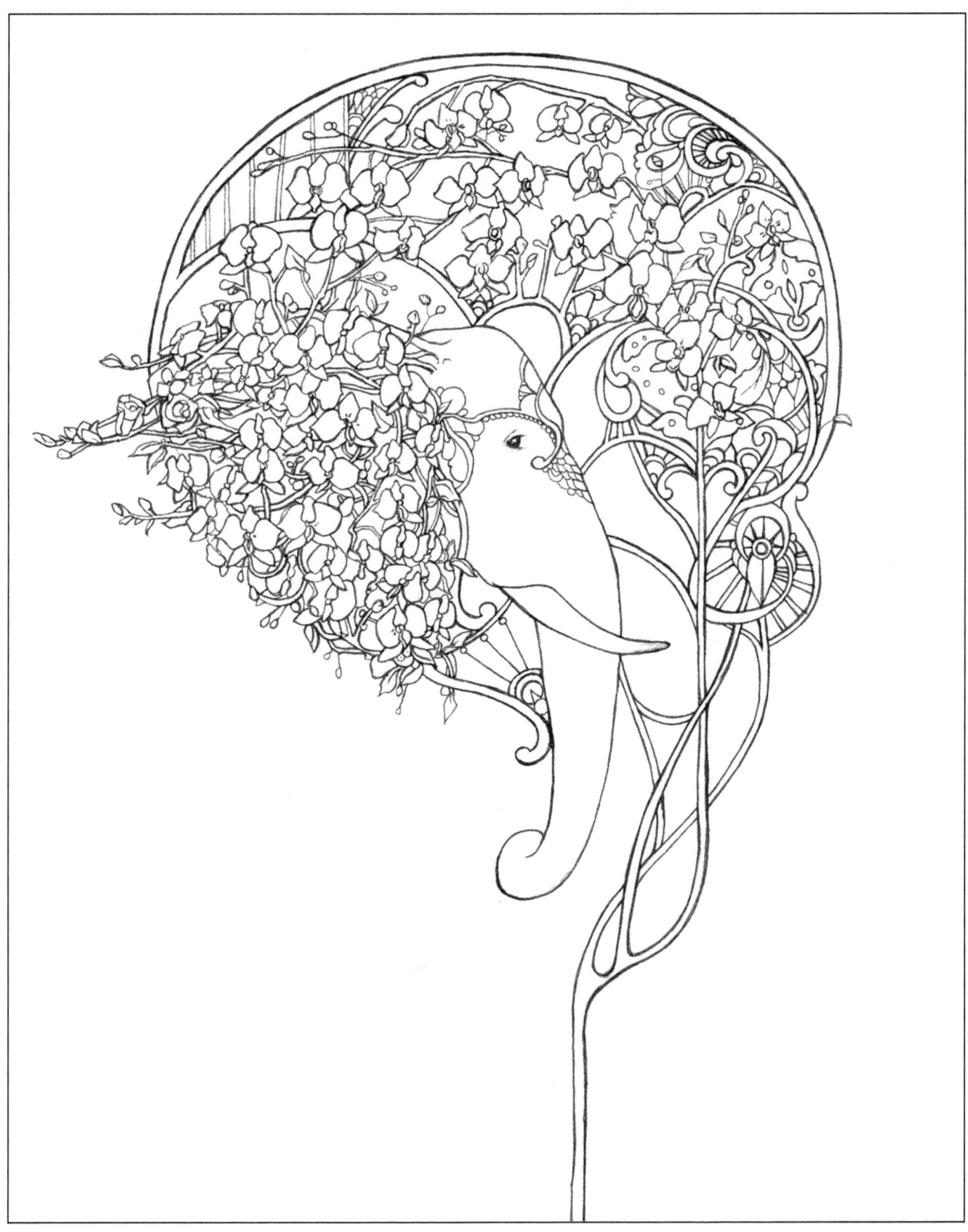

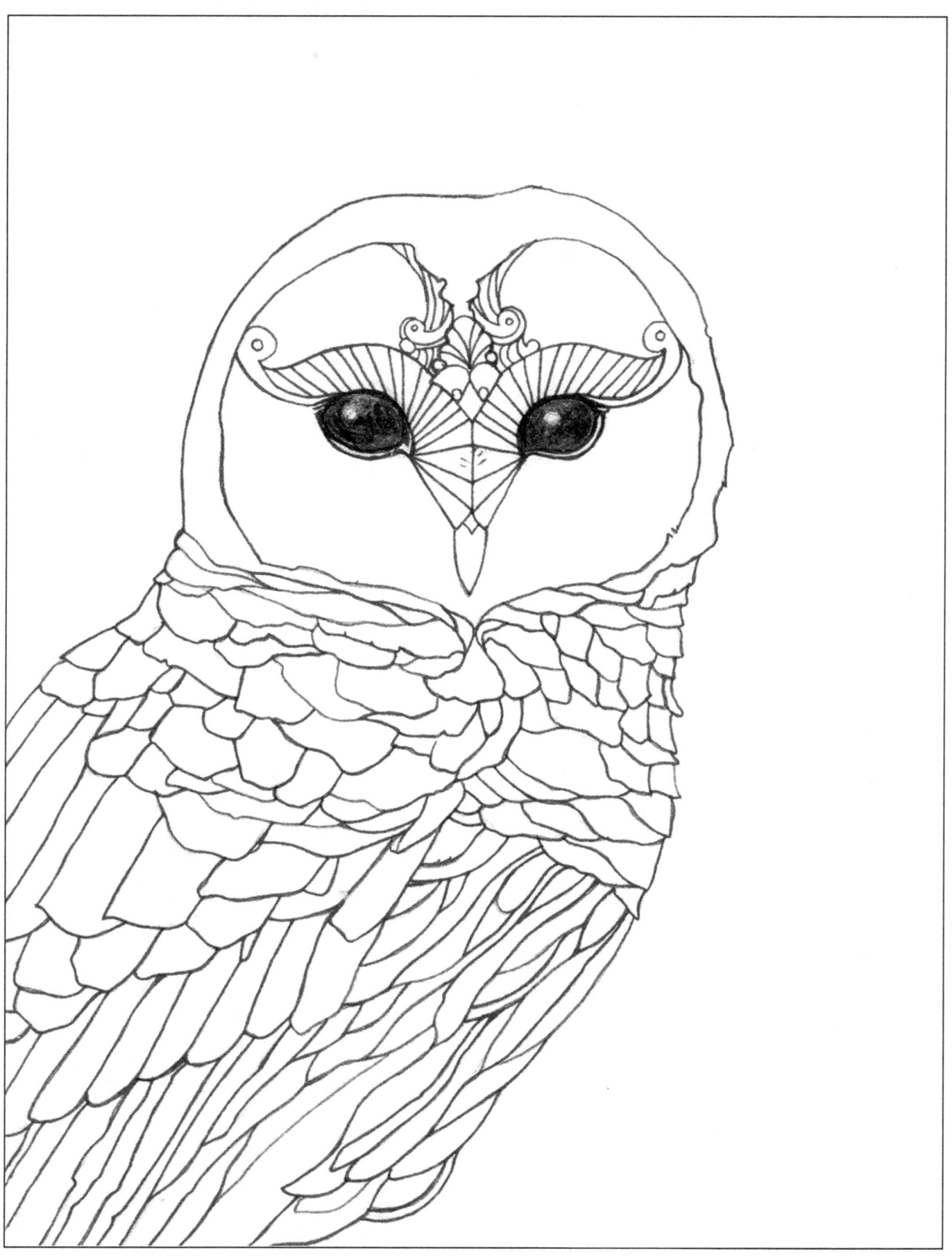

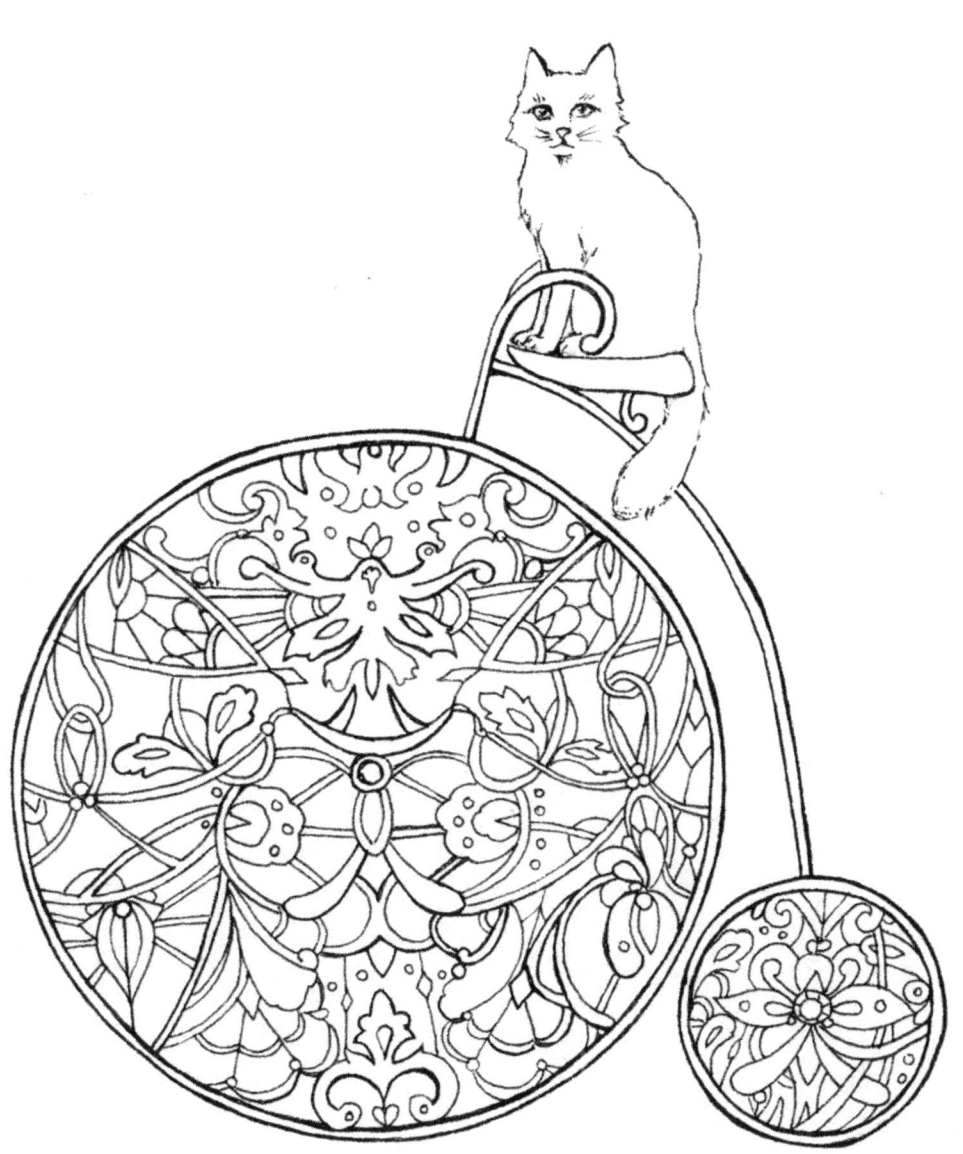

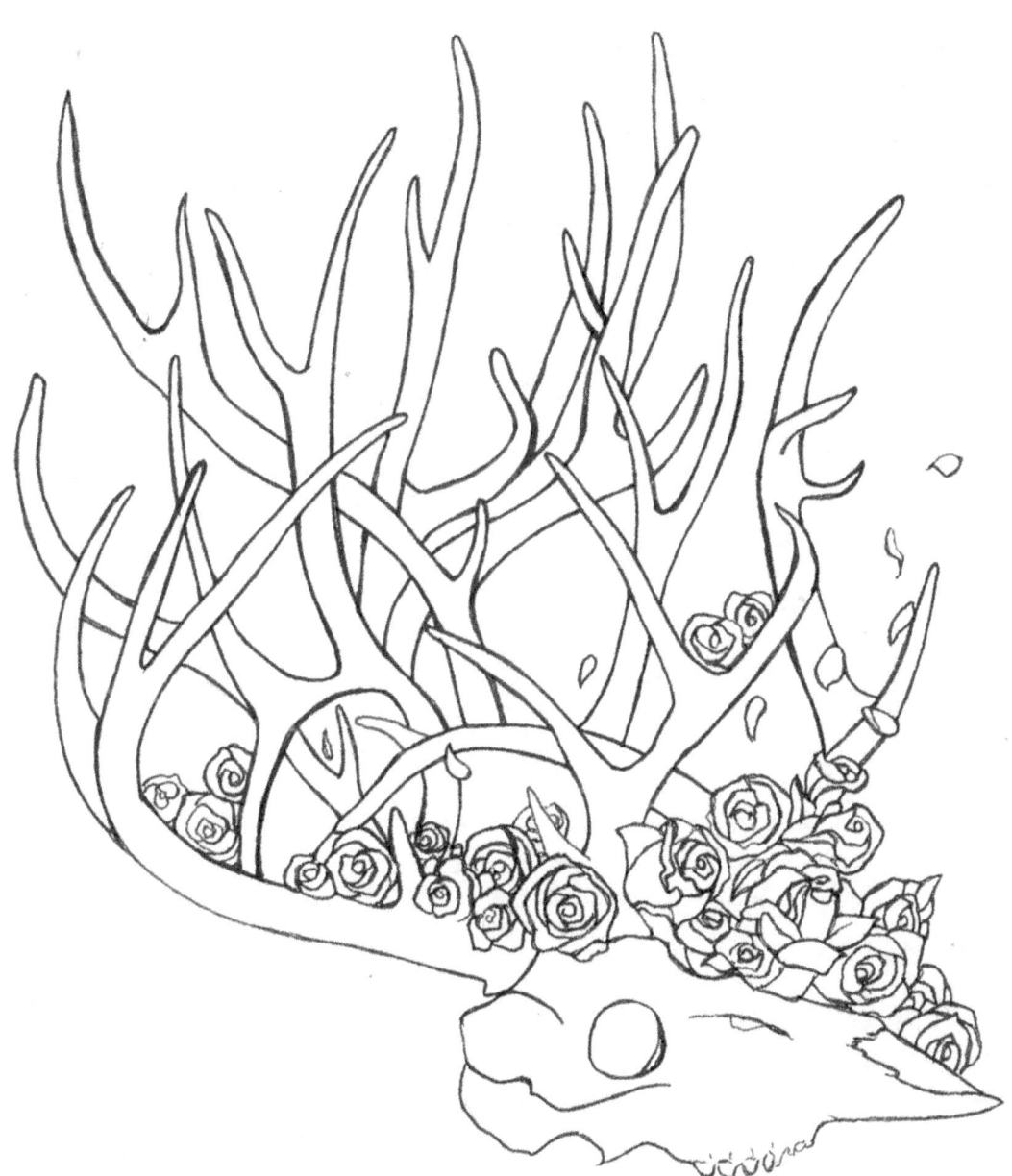

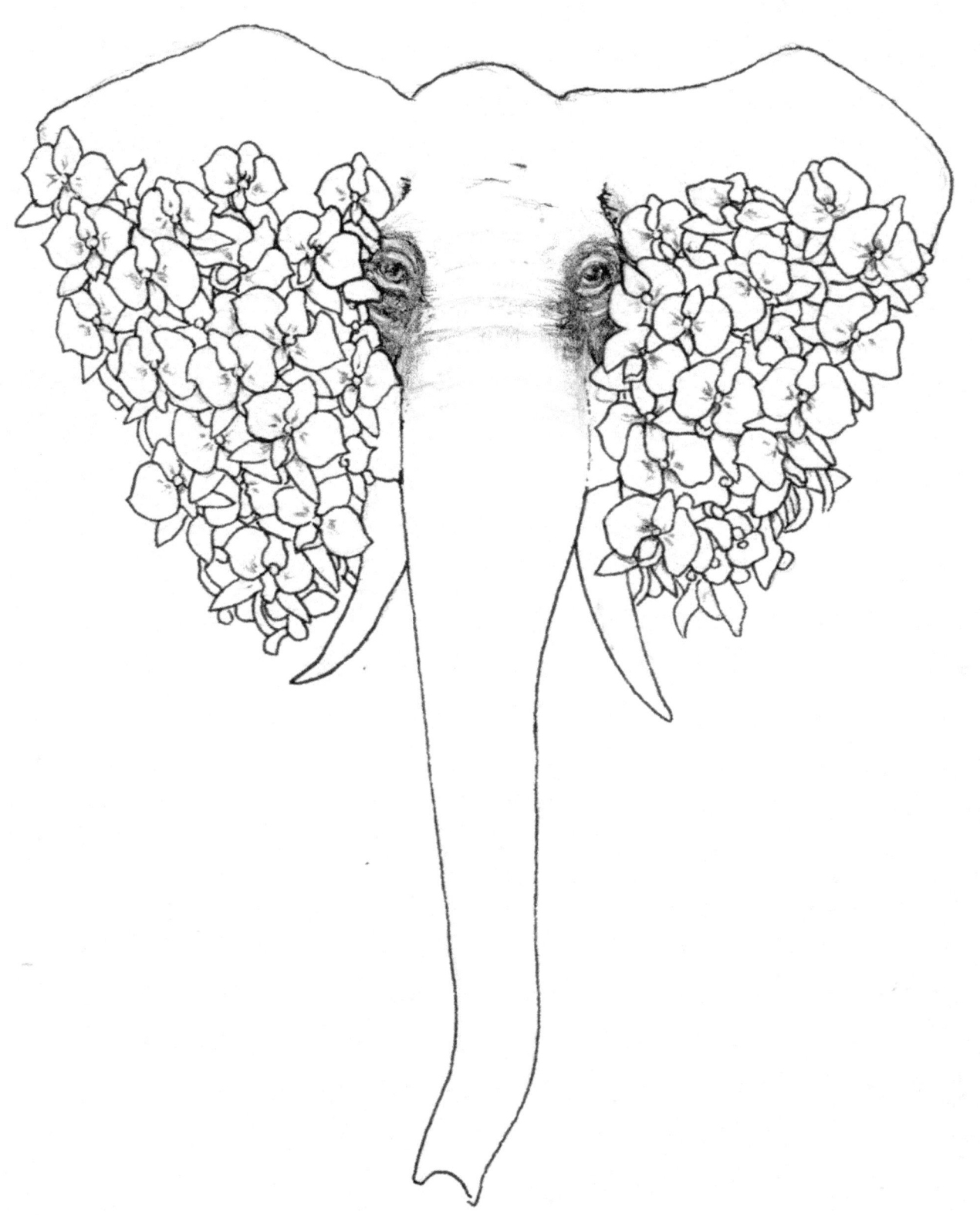

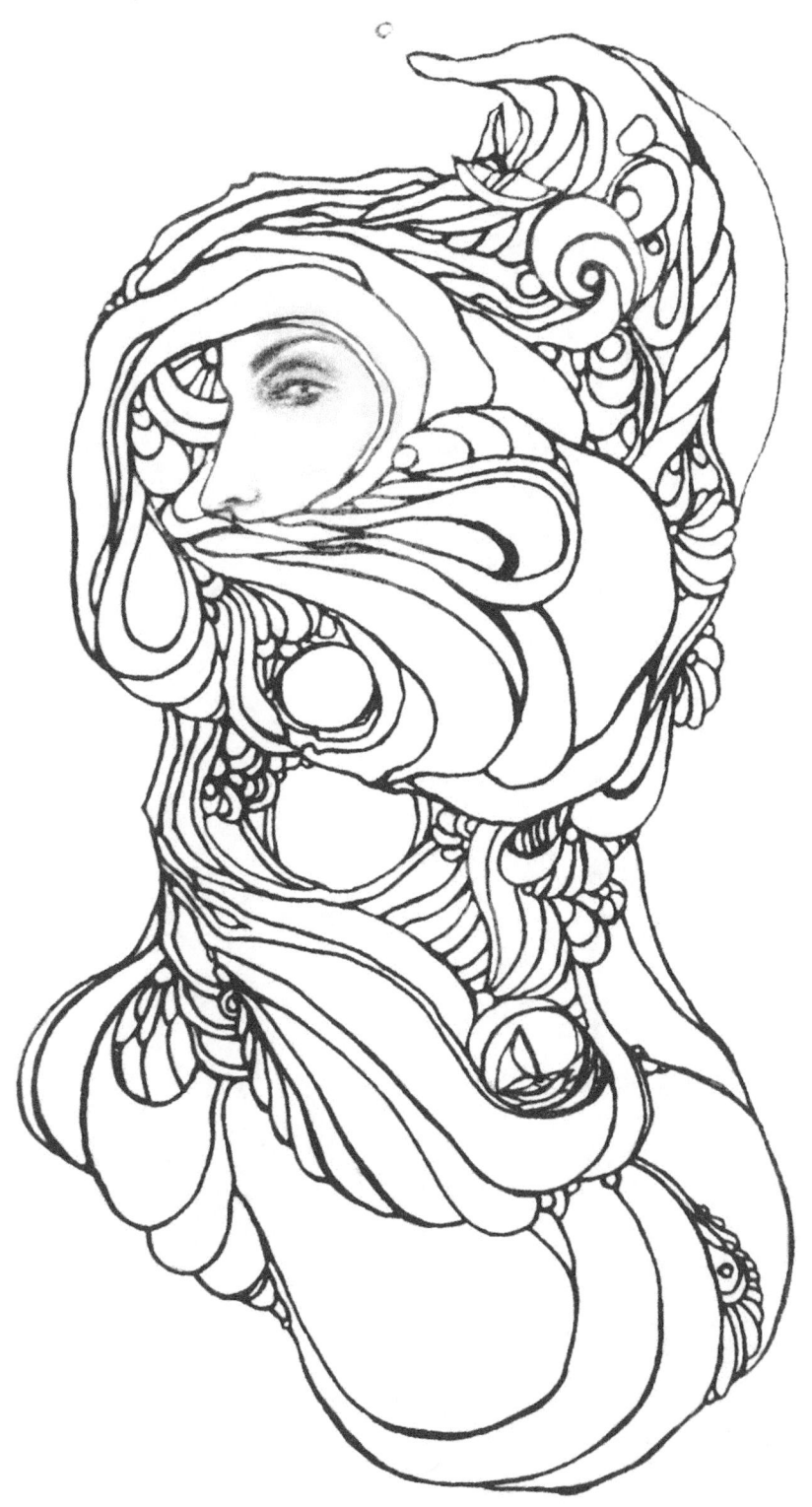

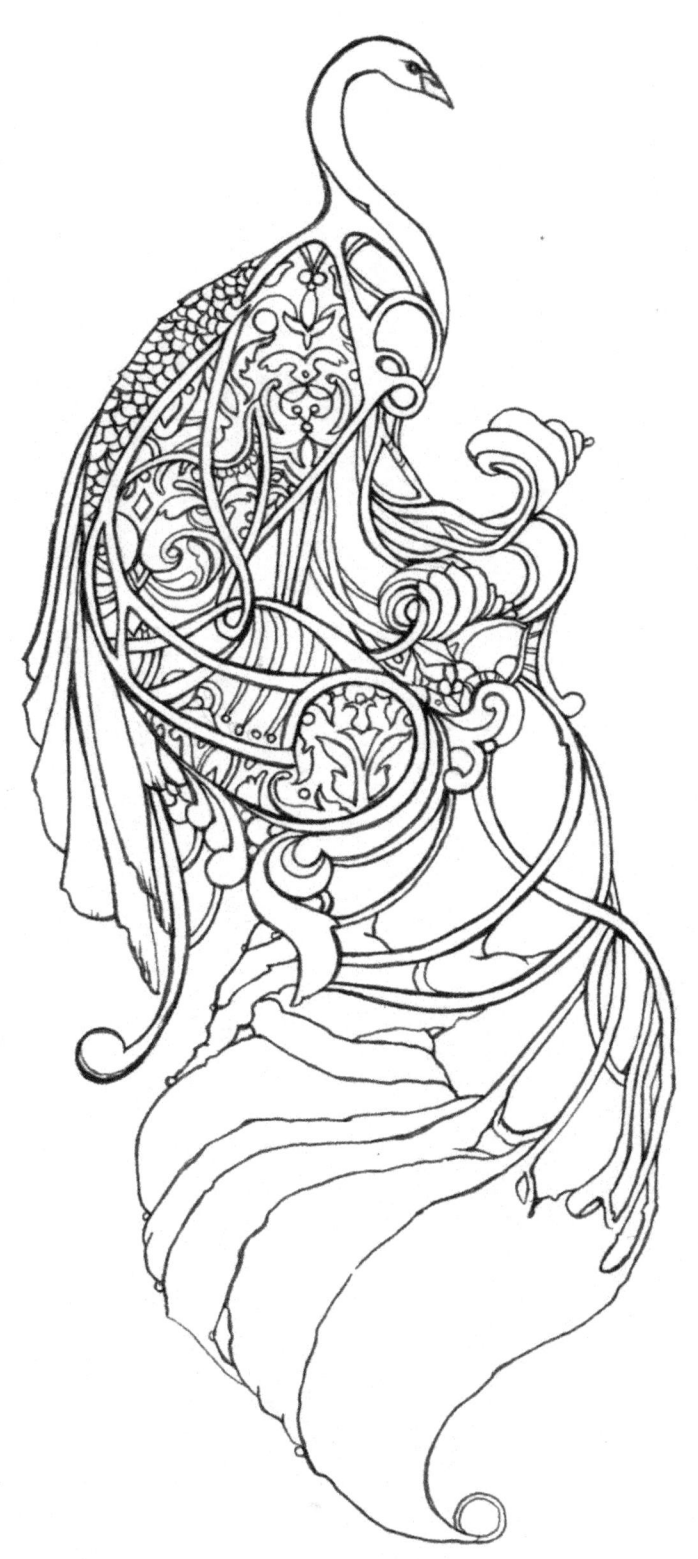

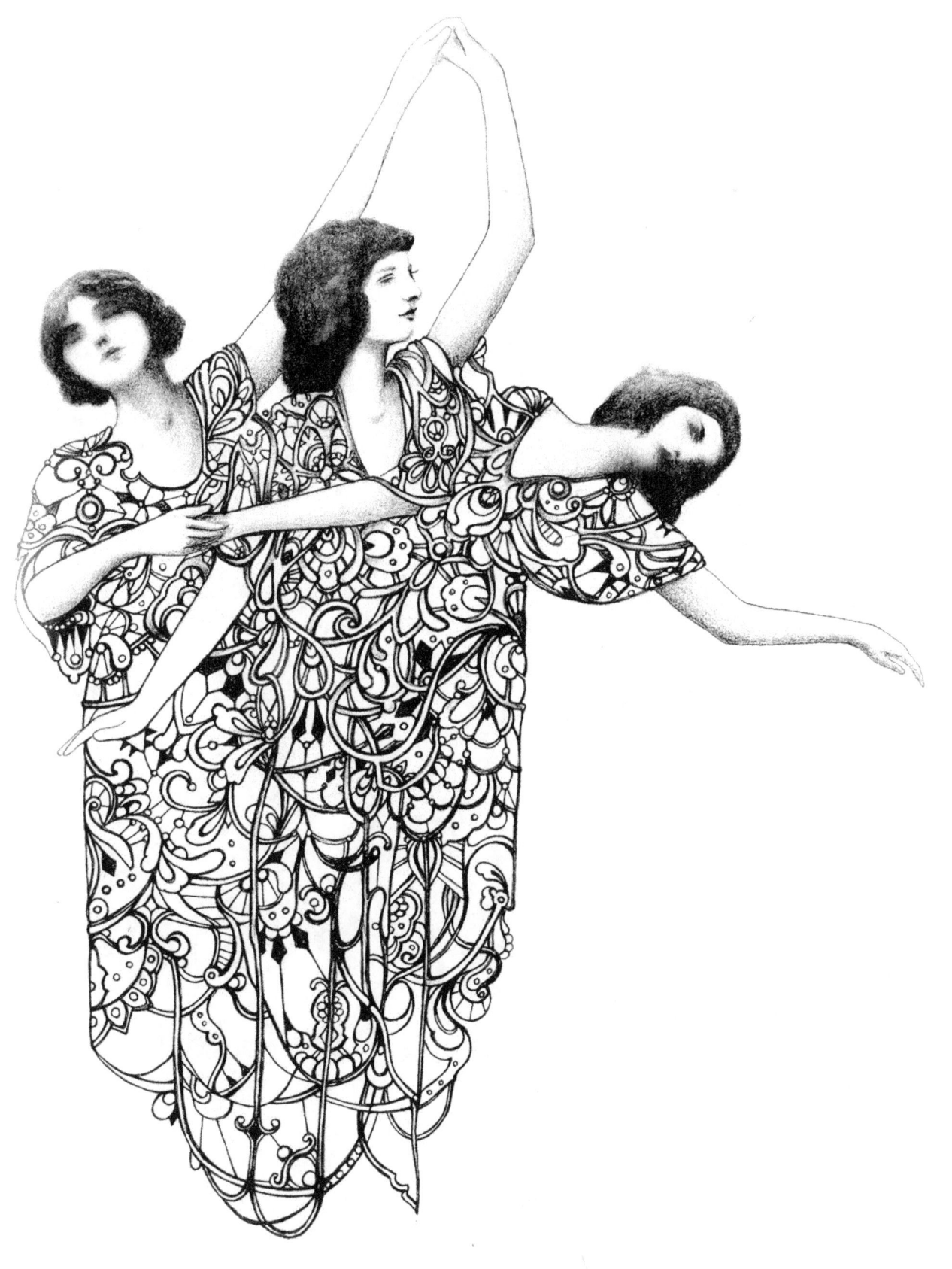

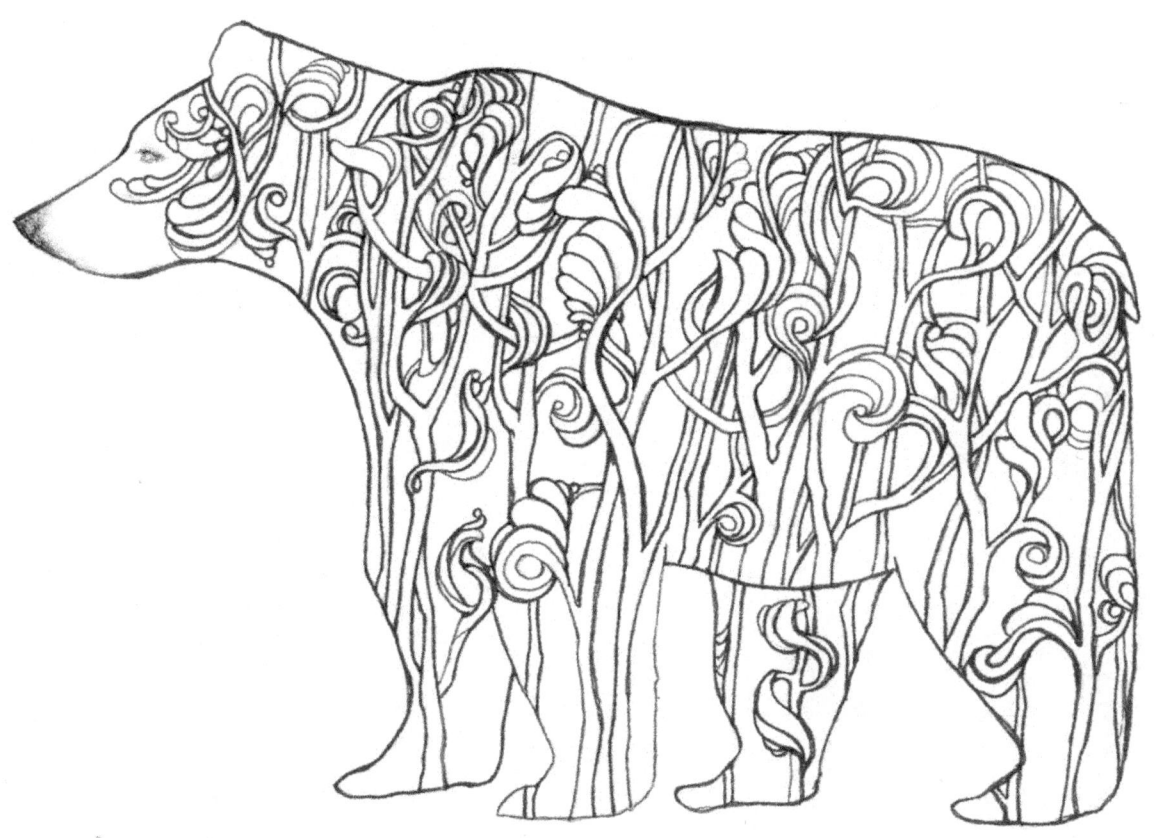

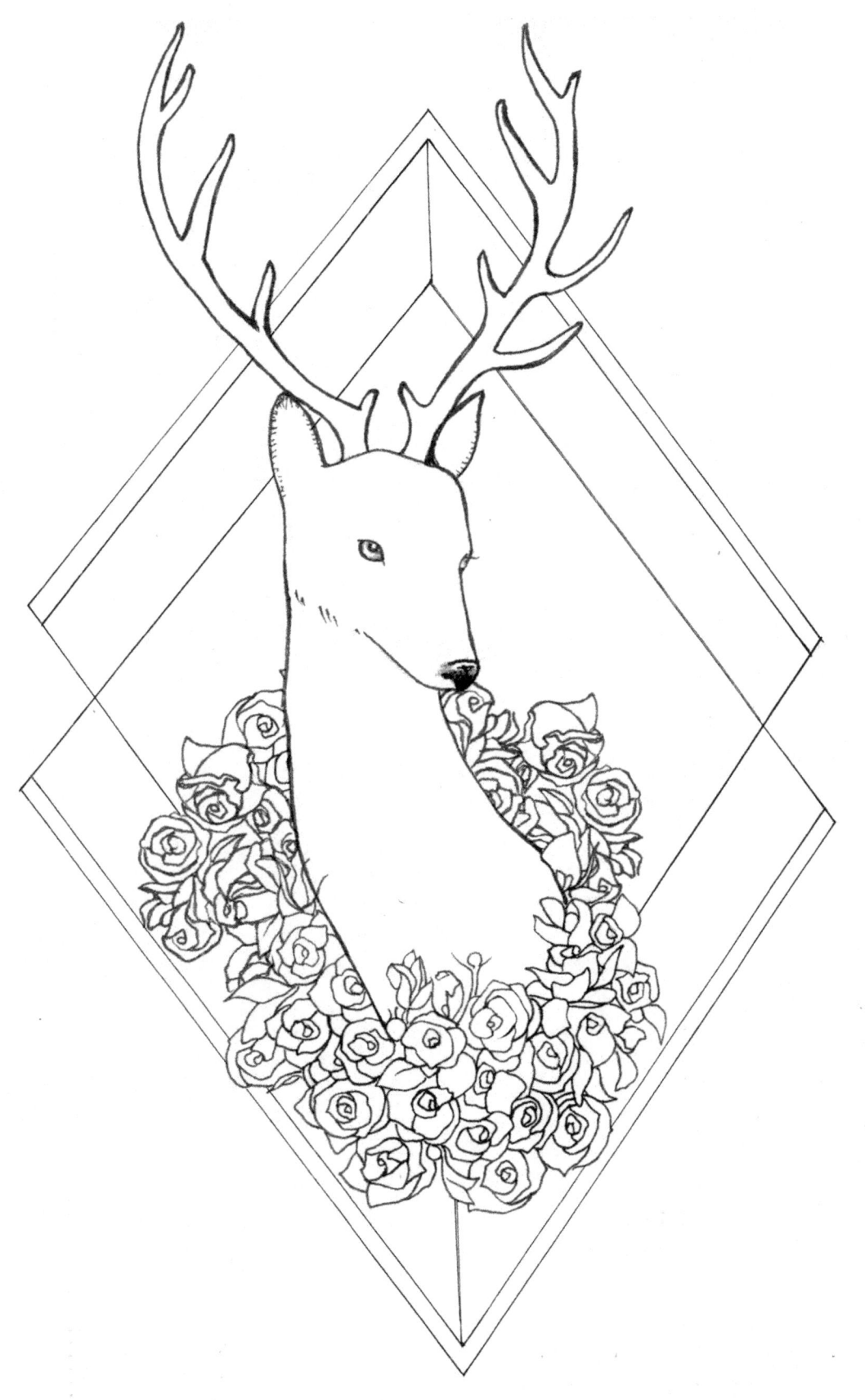

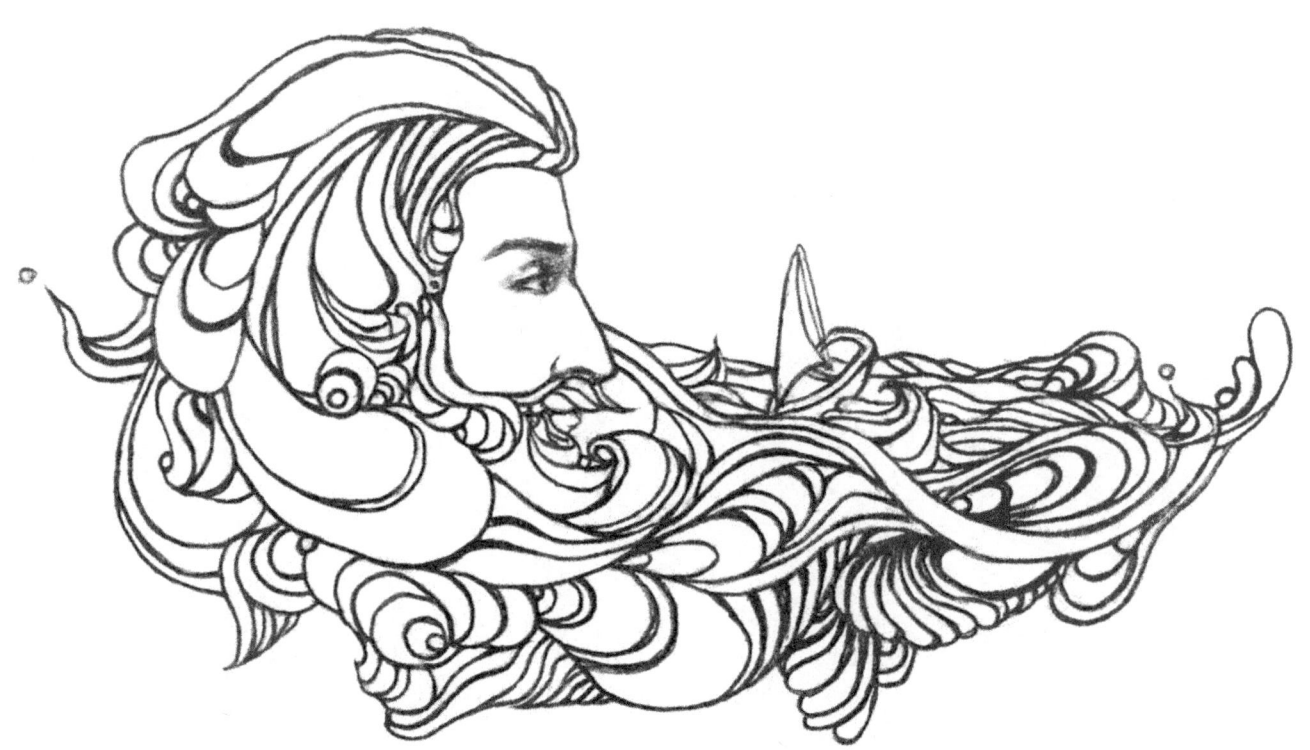

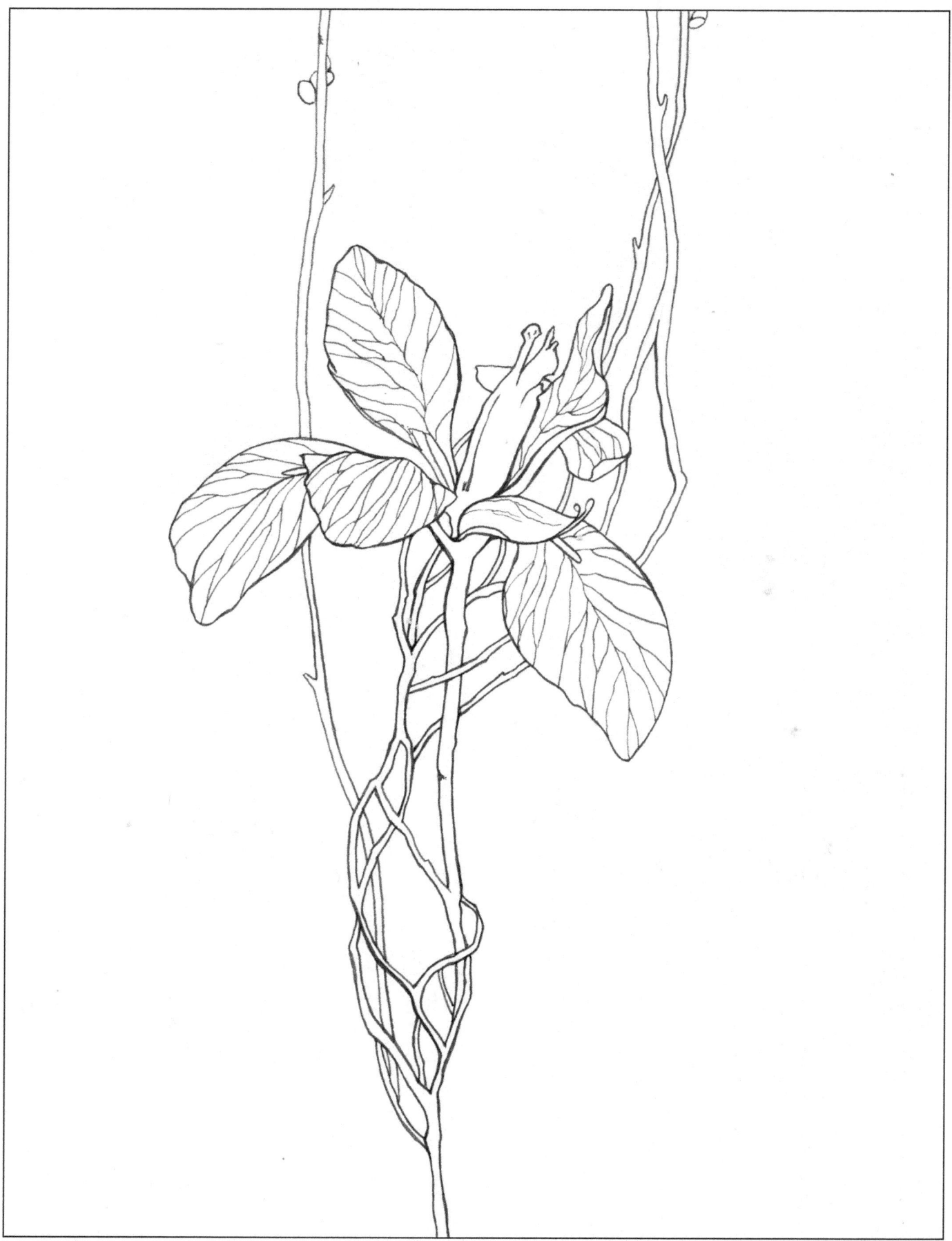

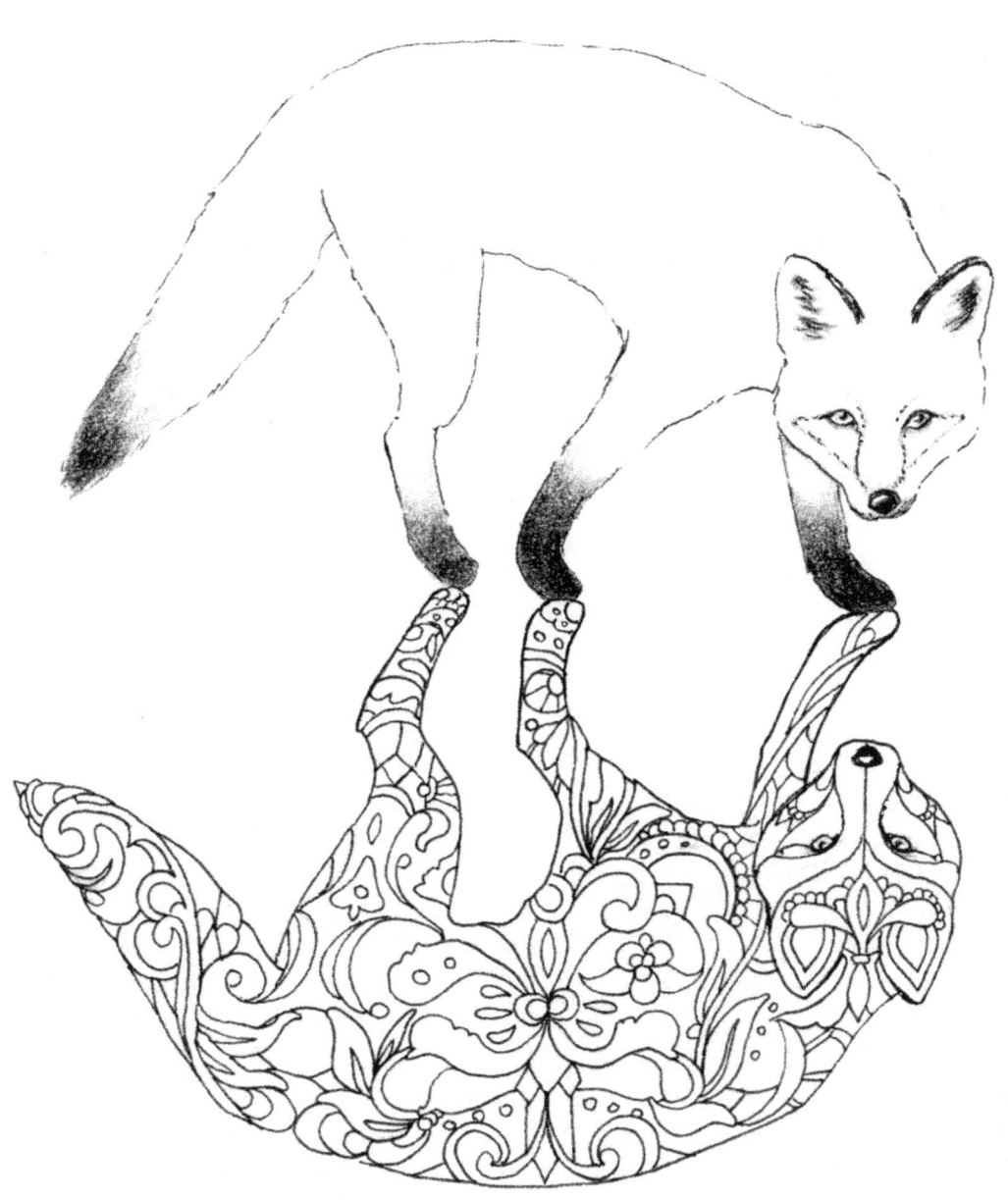

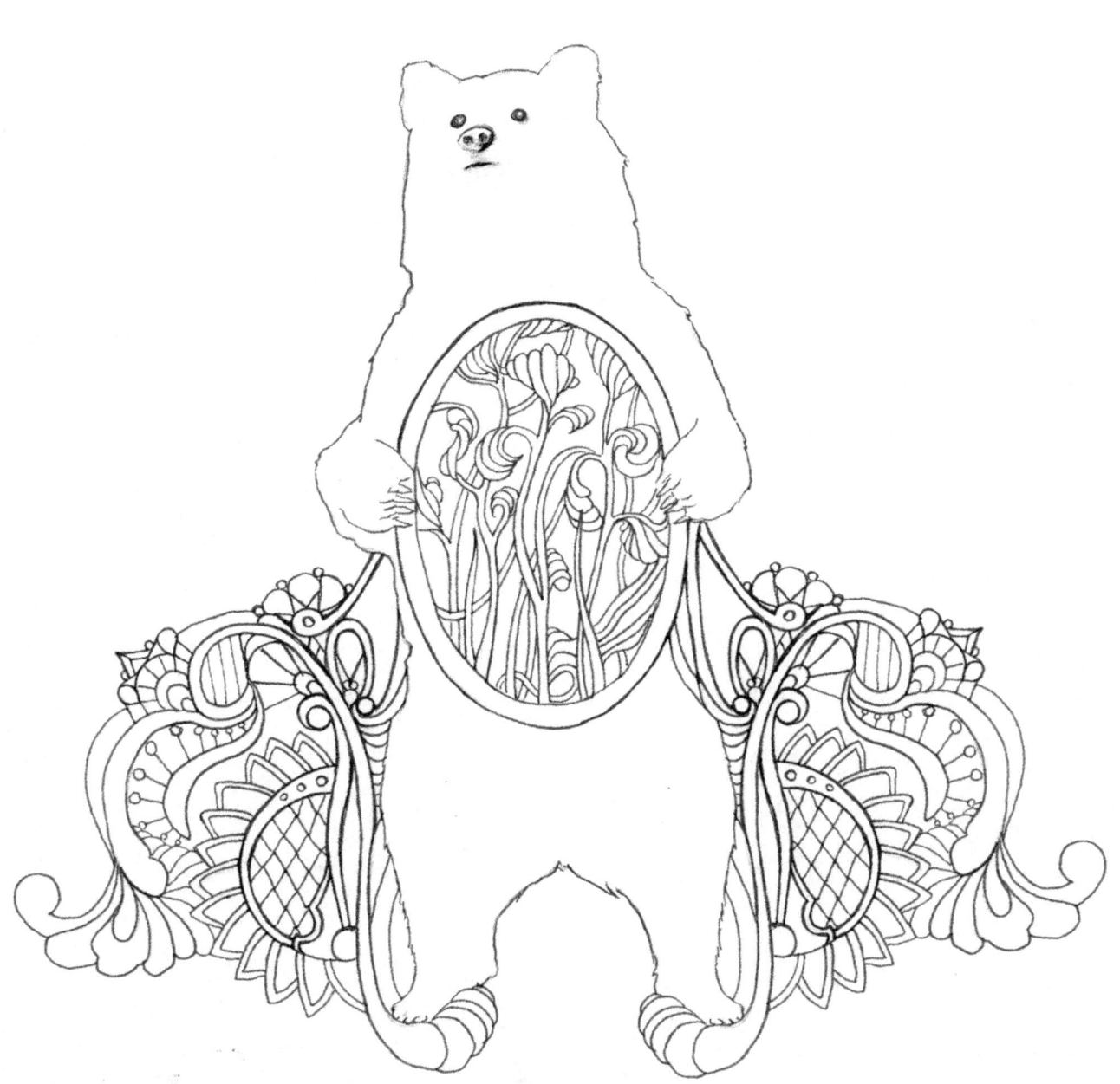

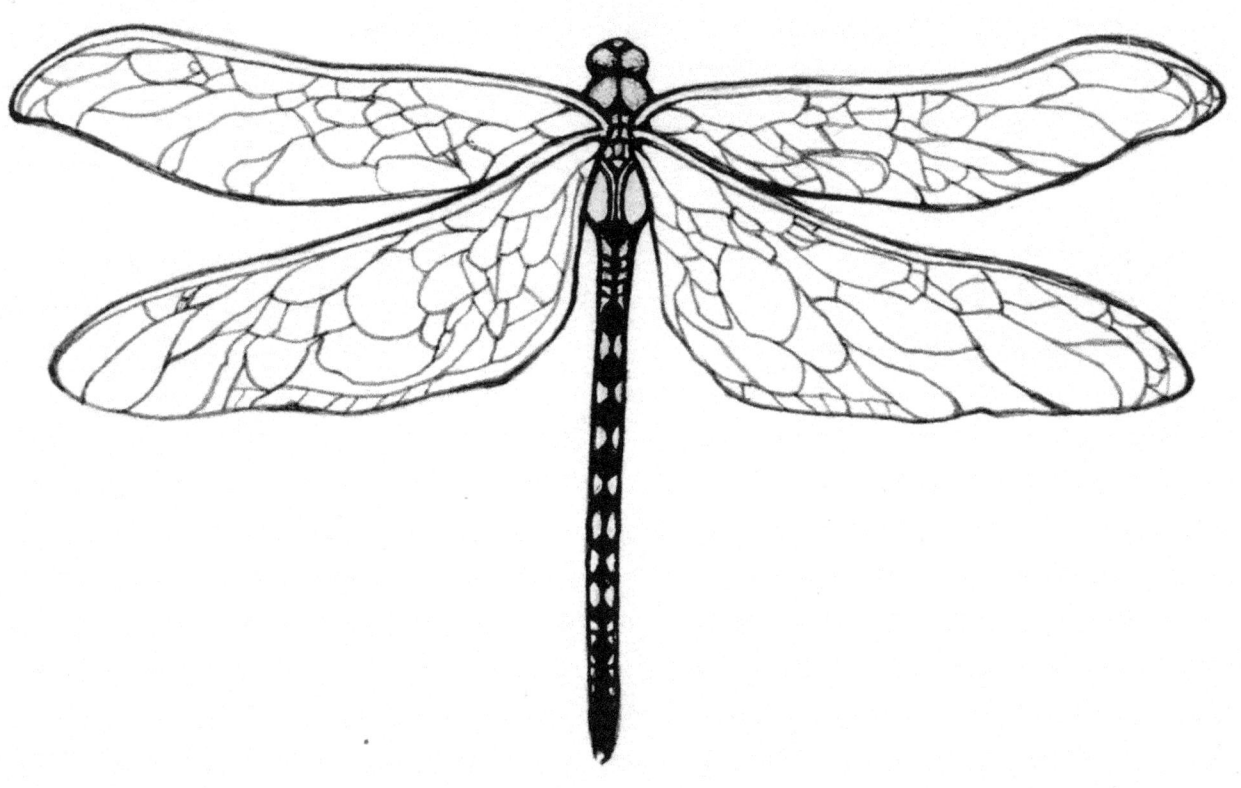

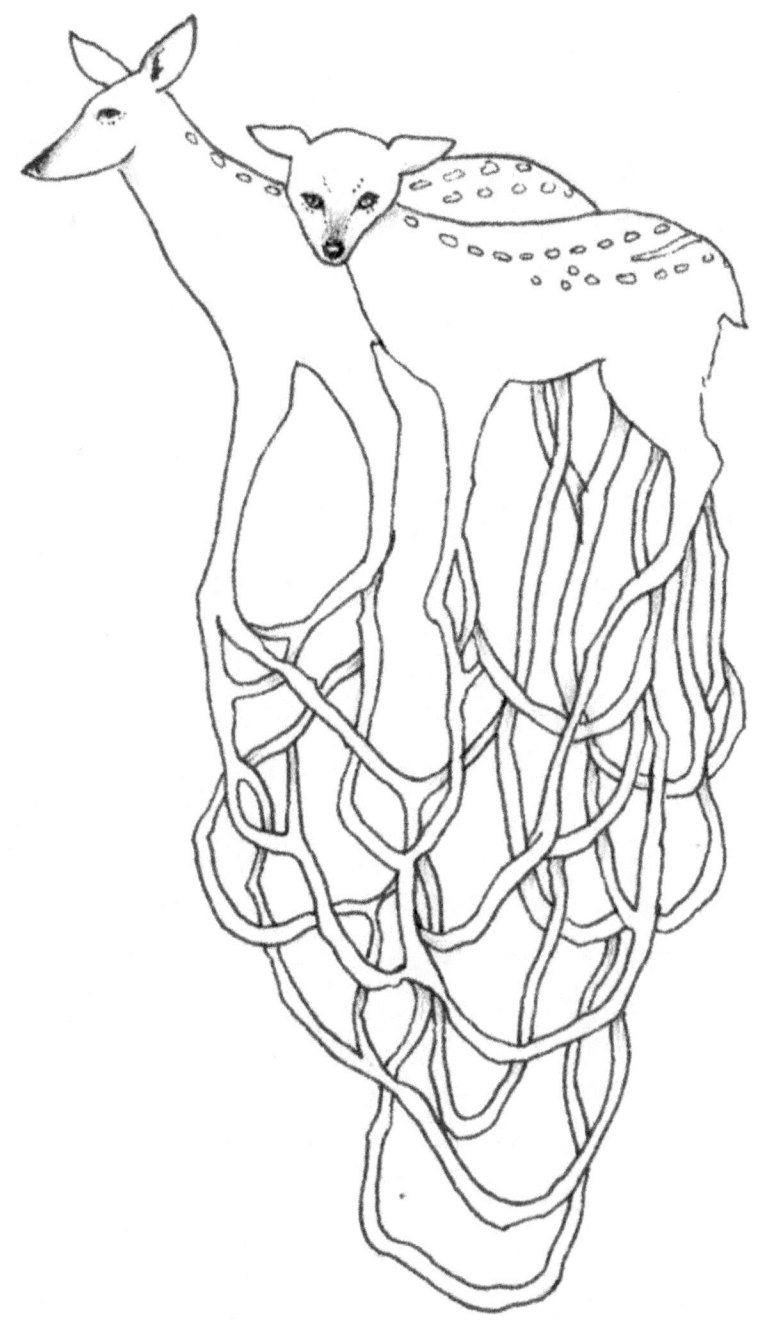

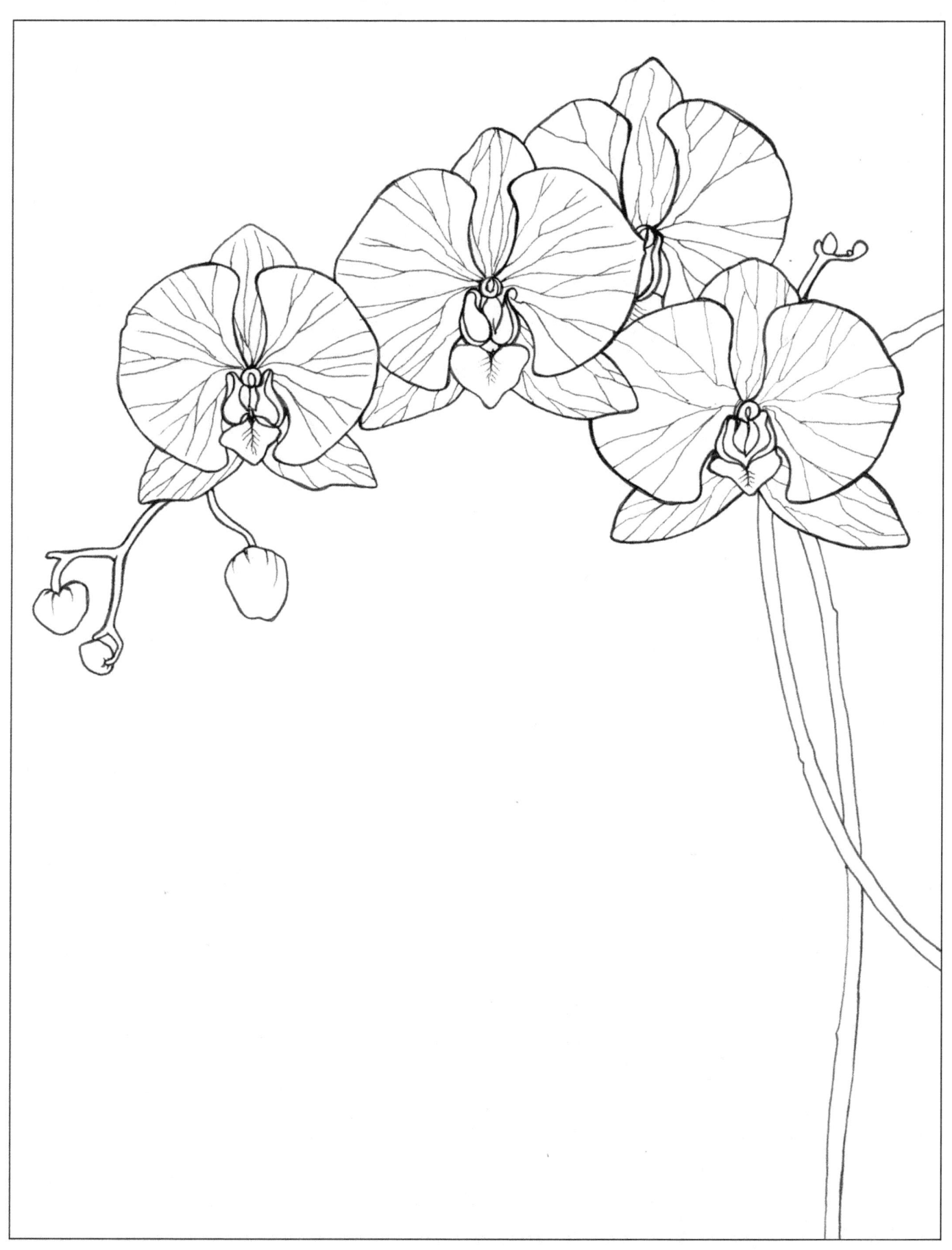

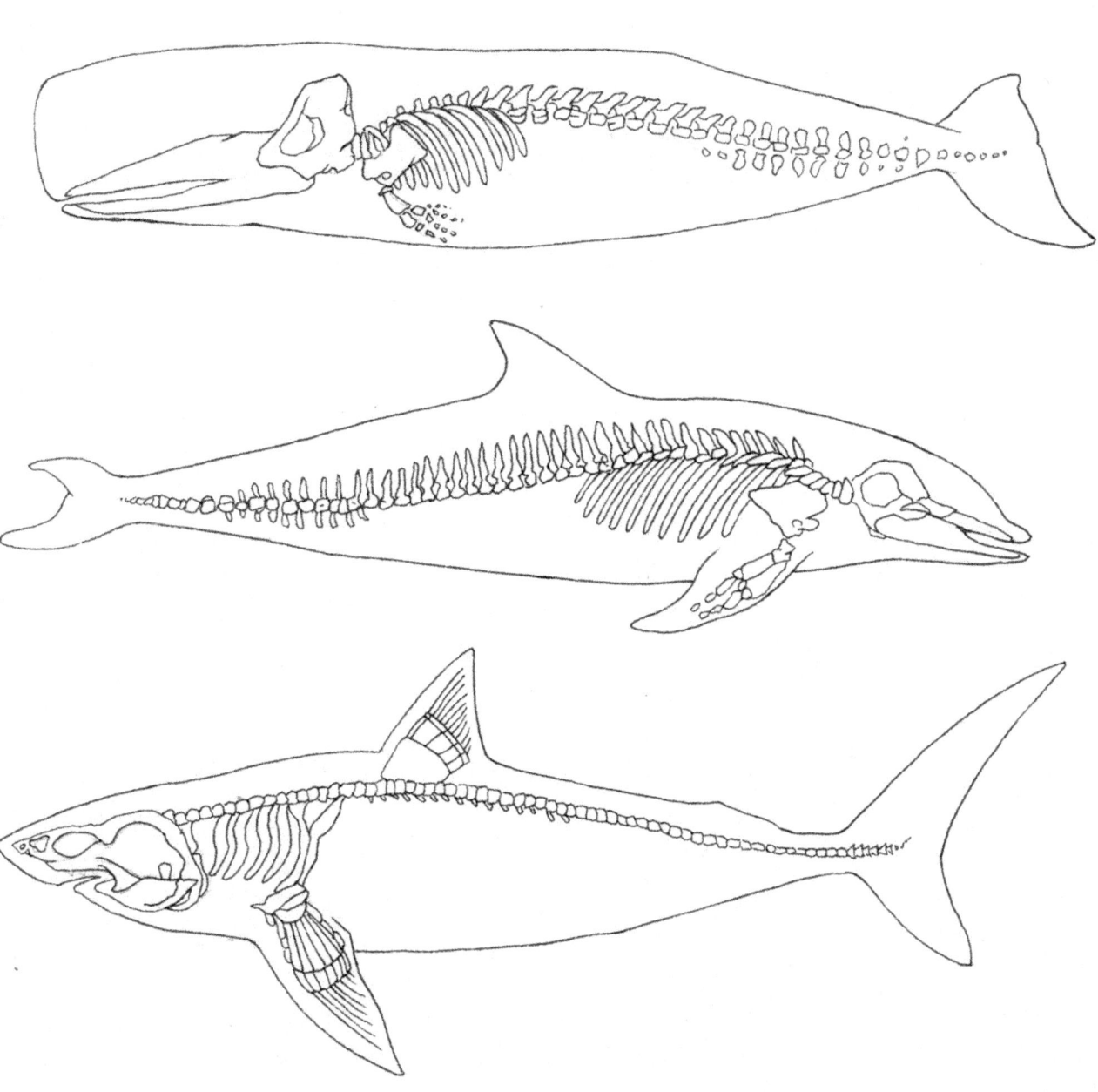

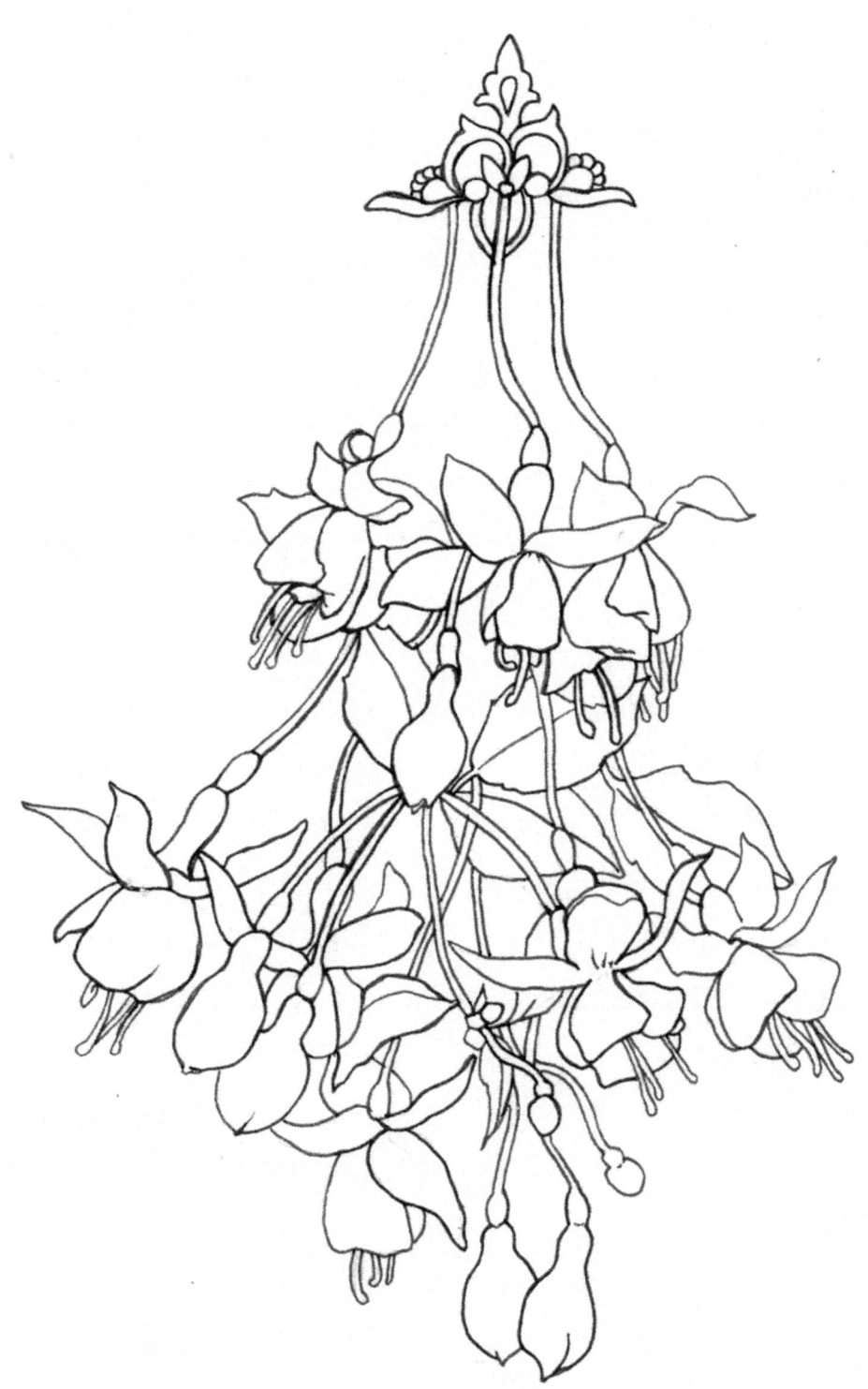

About the Artist

Liz Emirzian's career started at age 6, when she wrote her first book titled, *I Love Cats*. She strung together a hilariously imaginative sequence of illustrations that depicted all the things that cats can do. Liz continued her love for drawing, painting, and illustration into her adulthood, and received a Bachelors in Illustration from Ontario College of Art and Design University. Now, working out of New York City, she continues to create fine art and publications that speak to many people. You can see more of her work at www.lizemirzian.com.

More books from Kingfisher Press:

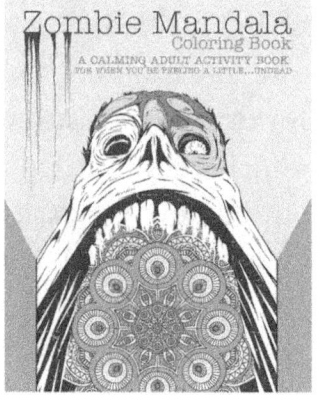

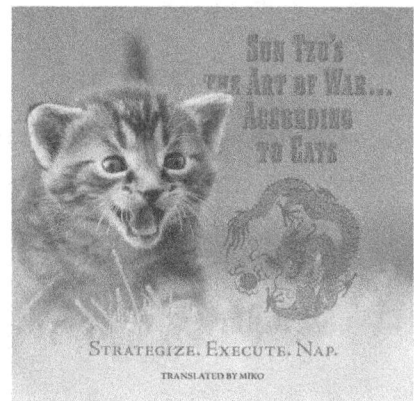

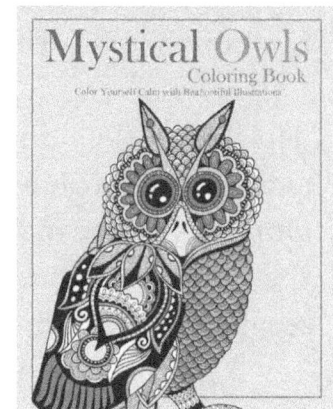

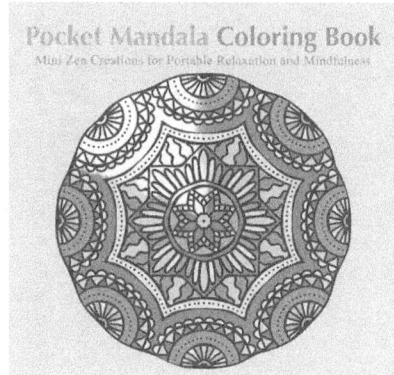

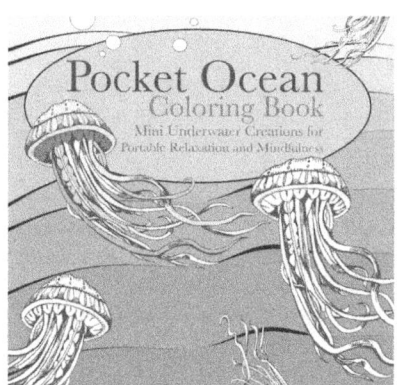

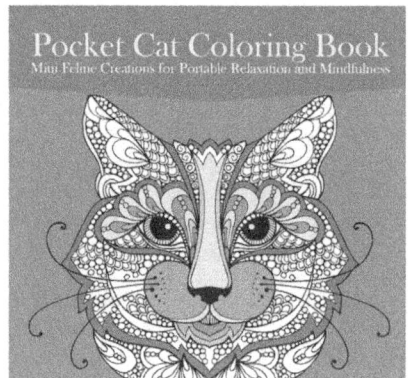

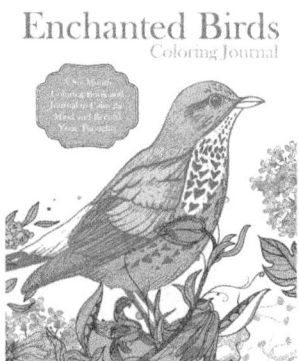

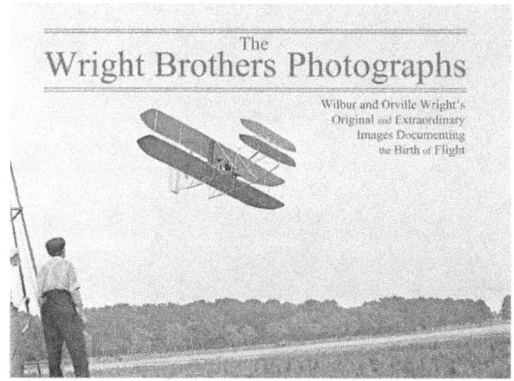

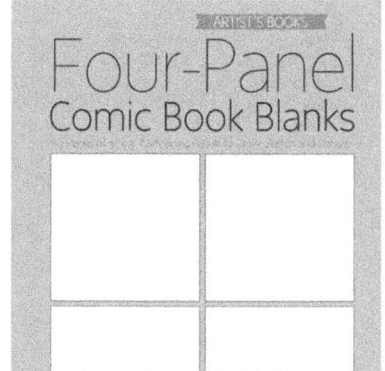

www.kingfisherpressbooks.com